And Through It All, HE KEPT ME

———— ❦ ————

BETTY BISHOP-CHAMBERS

ISBN 979-8-88540-399-3 (paperback)
ISBN 979-8-88540-400-6 (digital)

Copyright © 2022 by Betty Bishop-Chambers

All rights reserved. No part of this publication may be reproduced, distributed, or transmitted in any form or by any means, including photocopying, recording, or other electronic or mechanical methods without the prior written permission of the publisher. For permission requests, solicit the publisher via the address below.

Christian Faith Publishing
832 Park Avenue
Meadville, PA 16335
www.christianfaithpublishing.com

Printed in the United States of America

You shall eat the fruit of the labor
of your hands; you shall be blessed,
and it shall be well with you.

—Psalm 128:2 ESV

To my loving husband, Alvin Chambers Jr. whom I love dearly, who has listened to all my testimonies day after day, until one day he asked, "Why don't you write a book?" Even though I had a tugging on my heart to do it, I kept taking deep breaths, but I needed to hear it. I've not only heard it from him, but different people who have visited our church have spoken it, not directly to me but to the congregation. Alvin, I thank the Lord for your life and our lives together as my husband and friend and for encouraging me to write this book.

Contents

Preface xi
Acknowledgments xiii
Chapter 1: Lord, Don't Let Me Lose
            My Mind 1
Chapter 2: The Drawing/Salvation/
            Filled with Holy Spirit 4
            *How the Lord drew me
            (part 1)* 4
            Salvation (part 2) 6
            Speak in tongues 10
            A change has come over me 13
Chapter 3: Ask, Seek, Knock, and the
            Door Will Be Opened,
            Even in the Simple Things ... 14
            Peace and quiet 14
            A pair of shoes 15
            White sweater 16
            Missing debit card 16
            A Dress for the ball 17
            Washed my car 17

Chapter 4:	Forgiveness	20
	Witness/ex-husband	20
	A word of knowledge from "a true prophet"	22
Chapter 5:	Still, Small Voice—You Asked for That	25
Chapter 6:	Lord, You Give Me the Words to Say	29
Chapter 7:	Dreams	32
	The clouds rolled back	32
	The number seven	34
	Man of my dreams	35
	Wrong decision	35
	Dr. Gloria "Repent"	36
	A remarkable dream	38
Chapter 8:	Healing	42
	Asking God for direction in my life	43
	My fever broke	44
	Car radiator explosion	45
	Black rotting throat	46
	White spots	47
	The power of the Lord is in me!	47
	The party	49
	Caught in the trap	50

Chapter 9: Order My Steps
I Will Be at Your Side—
Instructing You, Leading
You, and Guiding You 54
$400 a week...........................55
The interview........................57
A clean slate 58
Lord, I need some help!..........60
Car worth $800 63
A new car...............................65
Never say never......................66
New lease 67
$1,100 down payment...........68
Chapter 10: Supernatural—The Blue
Armband Miracle 73
Chapter 11: Touch My Hand...................78
Chapter 12: The Title of This Book
and How It Came to Be 81
Chapter 13: Prayer for Salvation..............83

Preface

In my walk with the Lord, I have not always made the right decisions; however, I did not stay there. I got back up, dust myself off, and keep striving for the prize. I'm not saying we do wrong on purpose, just don't stay there. There is no one good but God.

I've used these, my testimonies of the Lord, to share the love, kindness, forgiveness, patience, and faithfulness of our Lord Jesus Christ.

I pray that this book is encouraging and an inspiration to those who read it and to those who hear it. May God continue to bless and keep you well.

"You're a good, good Father. That's who you are!"

> For a righteous man
> may fall seven times And rise

again but the wicked shall fall by calamity. (Proverbs 24:16 NKJV)

Do not rejoice when your enemy falls, And do not let your heart be glad when he stumbles. (Proverbs 24:17 NKJV)

Acknowledgments

To my Father God in heaven who has known me before I was formed in my mother's womb, who has loved me unconditionally, and given his life for me while I was still a sinner, who patiently waited for me to know him, who never put me down but built me up in his word. Putting people before me, speaking life into me, who kept me sane when I thought I would lose my mind, who was and is my friend when I had no friends. I love you, Lord, because you first loved me. Thank you, Father.

To my late mother, Rhoda Mae Jordan-Bishop, and my late father, George Bishop Sr., who brought me into this world. To my mother who raised all her children and a few grandchildren as a single parent, thank you for loving us and keeping us all together in the house that my dad bought for us, for taking us to church, and for sending us to church even when you could not go. I miss you so much, and I love you twice as much. Love you, Madea.

To my late father whom I met but did not know, thank you for putting my mom in her own home before leaving us. I love you for that, Dad.

To my church, a real church, Jesus People Ministries Church—that when I asked the Lord to "send me to a real church," he *showed* me this church—thank you for being right where God needed you to be.

To my pastors and founders, the late bishop Isaiah S. Williams, founder; Dr. Gloria Y. Williams, cofounder; and my senior pastor, Richelle Lorde, all of whom I have the utmost respect for, whom I will continue to follow after as they continue to follow after Christ—thank you. I love you and thank you for the love you all pour out on us.

To all the people whom God has put in my life, who has made these testimonies possible, and whose names I have changed—thank you.

1

Lord, Don't Let Me Lose My Mind

God makes his sun rise on me and sent his rain on me even when I didn't know him. He loved me.

Before being born again, I was going through so much hurt, pain, and stress in my life with my now ex-husband Jessie. I thought I was going to lose my mind. I did not eat, comb my hair, bathe, or sleep; I just could not take care of myself.

One day, at his mother's house, I was talking to her, and as I was passing a mirror and happened to turn and look in it and saw myself, I stopped in my tracks. I had gone from a size 9 to a size 0. (I didn't know they made a size 0.) I was dirty; my hair was not combed; I was skinny, tired, hungry.

I began to cry seeing myself like that. With my hands on my face, I said, "Betty, Look at you!" Then I cried out, "*Lord, don't let me lose my mind.*" At that very moment, I felt peace come over me. I went home, took a bath, washed my hair, ate, lay down, and went to sleep.

When Jessie came home from being out for several nights, he woke me up and asked, "What's wrong with you?" as he poked me in my back continually with his finger. (Normally, I was up all night, crying, looking out of the window every time a car went by).

"Man, get in the bed and go to sleep, and let me go back to sleep," I said. He didn't stop. However, what he did not know was I had an encounter with the Lord, and nothing he did anymore fazed me. I called on the Lord. He heard my cry and answered. I had been delivered! I praise you, Lord!

After I received salvation, I was reading Romans 10:13: "For whosoever shall call upon the name of the Lord shall be saved." I began to cry because I realized that I'm a "whosoever," and he saved me. God knows our hearts. Thank you, Lord.

> For there is no difference between the Jew and the Greek: for the same Lord over all is rich unto all that call upon him. (Romans 10:12 KJV)

> And it shall come to pass, that whosoever shall call on the name of the Lord shall be saved. (Acts 2:21 KJV)

> But the Lord said to Samuel "Do not look at his appearance or at his physical stature because I have refused him. For the Lord does not see as man sees, for man looks at the outward appearance but the Lord looks at the heart." (1 Samuel 16:7 NKJV)

2

The Drawing/Salvation/ Filled with Holy Spirit

How the Lord drew me (part 1)

God knows the place, the day, the hour, down to the second when our hearts are ready to receive him. I had been working on my job for about two years when I decided to change jobs. After being gone for about three months on the new job, I realized it was not for me.

I called my former supervisor and asked for my job back. She said yes. I went to HR so I could get back into the system. The lady told me, "You've never been taken out of the system." Praise the Lord. I did not lose any of the two years I had worked. So when I went back to the unit, a new employee had been transferred there, and he and my friend Belle had become close.

Every night I would hear them talking about the Lord and all the stories of the Bible, just really enjoying themselves and praising the Lord.

I was enjoying it too. I wanted to know about all these people they were talking about. I would sit close enough to hear what they were saying but far enough away so they don't ask me any questions because I did not know anything. This went on for a couple of months.

Well, I couldn't just sit there and hear about all those wonderful people they were talking about. I wanted to be a part of it. So one morning, when I got off from work, I went to the Bible bookstore, bought myself a Bible, and began reading it. That night, when I got to work, I finished my work, walked through the doorway, and said, "Let me tell you about the story I read." They looked up at me and listened. I don't remember what I read, but I was so excited to be able to share a story with them and eager to listen to theirs. This went on every night for a while.

> No man can come to me; except the Father which hath sent me draw him: and I will raise him up at the last day. (John 6:44 KJV)

> Jesus said unto him, I am the way, the truth, and the life: no man cometh unto the Father, but by me. (John 14:6 KJV)

Salvation (part 2)

Every morning at work, at 4:00 a.m., some of my coworkers would go to the chapel on their break and have church service. One morning, Margaret invited me. I went, and each night, for a while after that, I continued to go.

This particular morning, Margaret; Belle; Eunice, our supervisor; and I were in service this time. After service, when we were praying out, my supervisor began speaking in an unknown language. As we were leaving, I asked Belle, "What was she doing?"

"Speaking tongues," she said. I asked, "Can anybody understand it?"

"No," she said. "Nobody but God."

When we got back to the unit at 5:00 a.m., my supervisor called me to the office. When I walked in, she and Margaret were there. She asked me if I wanted to receive Jesus as my Lord and Savior. "Yes," I said. I repeated the words that she said, and they hugged me and welcomed me into the body of Christ. I knew what I said; however, I guess I was looking for something to happen, and it did. I got home about 8:00 a.m. that Saturday morning. I got on my knees and said, "Lord, if somebody can talk to you from here all the way up there, it's got to be good. I wanna talk to you just like that. Lord, send me to a real church."

I left the house, but I don't remember where I went that morning nor where I was coming from, nevertheless, I was coming back home. And as I was driving on 826 Expressway, just as I got in front of this particular building, the Lord prompted me to look to my right. And I saw this church—Jesus People Ministries Church. As I continued driving, I found myself saying, "Jesus People, Jesus People, I'm Jesus People." As I pulled into the yard, I had gotten the revelation: "I am Jesus People." I did not know where this church was, but God showed it to me.

I was back home now and called Grace, my former beautician who was a member there, but she had not been attending. Every time she did my hair, she would always talk about the church and how the pastor there could surely preach. Anyway, I asked her if she "would go the church with me tomorrow (Sunday)?"

"Yes," she said. (By the way, Grace told me that I was the one who started her going back to church again.) Glory to God!

I went to work that night, and I was telling all my coworkers I was going to church on Sunday (in the morning). Everyone was excited for me. Margaret said, "Something is going to happen to you even better." The day shift came in, and I began sharing it with Clair (who is also a Christian). As she was staring at me, she asked, "What church are you going to?"

"Jesus People," I said.

Staring, she said, "They don't speak in tongues there."

I just smiled. I really didn't know what she was talking about, nor did I care. All I know was, I had this *urgent* stirring in my belly that I had to go to church that morning, and I had to go to that church.

> But what saith it? The word is nigh thee, even in thy mouth, and in thy heart: that is, the word of faith which we preach; (Romans 10:8 KJV)

> That if thou shalt confess with thy mouth the Lord Jesus, and believe in thine heart that God raised him from the dead, thou shalt be saved. (Romans 10:9 KJV)

> For with the heart man believeth unto righteousness; and with the mouth confession is made unto salvation. (Romans 10:10 KJV)

Baptized with Holy Spirit (part 3)
Speak in tongues

That Sunday morning, I got home, got dressed for church, picked up Grace and her husband, and went to church. There was a visiting pastor that Sunday. After he finished preaching, he had an altar call. One of the calls was, "How many of you have never spoken in tongues?" I raised my hand (along with others), and he told us to come down to the altar.

He turned the service back over to the pastor. He prayed, then said, "Close your eyes. Open your mouth. No matter what comes out, don't worry about it or how weird it may sound, just open your mouth." Then he called all the elders of the church to the altar, and they all began speaking in tongues.

I was standing there with my mouth closed, and I was trying to peek to see what all that noise was, even though I had my head slightly bowed.

All of a sudden, I heard a delicate whisper in my left ear that said, "Open your mouth." My mouth then opened in a gasp and immediately began speaking in tongues. The voice sounded like the pastor's, so I thought he had come down from the platform. However, when I opened my mouth, I also opened my eyes, and the pastor was still on the platform. Oh, my knees and legs became like rubber. I felt somebody's hands underneath my arms. I felt like I had been drinking. When Holy Spirit released me, I had been taken to a room within the church. Someone asked me if I knew "what just happened to me." I opened my mouth to speak, and I was still speaking in tongues. They told me I was "baptized with the Holy Ghost with the evidence of speaking tongues."

I was off that night, so I had to wait until my shift came in at 11:00 p.m. to call them to share the good news. They were all excited, except for my friend Belle. I was so excited. I began telling everybody everything that was happening in my life regarding the Lord.

> And suddenly there came a sound from heaven as of a rushing mighty wind, and it filled all the house where they were sitting. (Acts 2:2 KJV)

> And they were filled with Holy Ghost, and began to speak with other tongues, as the Spirit gave them utterance. (Acts 2:4 KJV)

> And when Paul placed his hands on them; and they spake with tongues, and prophesied. (Acts 19:6 KJV)

> For he that speaketh in an unknown tongue speaketh not unto men, but unto God: for no man understandeth him; howbeit in the

spirit he speaks mysteries. (1 Corinthians 14:2 KJV)

A change has come over me

The following Sunday, I went to church, and the choir sang "A Change." As soon as I heard those words, my body raised up, and I was standing to my feet, with my hands raised, my fingers stretched out as if I could touch the ceiling. There was such a great stirring in my belly that I had to take in tremendous amounts of air just to push out the words "Yes, Lord! Yes, Lord! Yes, Lord." It seemed as if I was trying to extinguish or quench that fire deep inside my stomach. When I sat back down, I wondered, what happened? I also joined the church that day, and the next time, they called for water baptism. I was baptized.

3

Ask, Seek, Knock, and the Door Will Be Opened, Even in the Simple Things

Peace and quiet

My son, James, and I were living with my sister and one of her daughters. James and I had just gotten home from church that evening, and I had to work that night. So I needed to get some rest. I was exhausted.

My nephew had come over, and he, my sister, and my niece were all in the living room, talking loud, cussing (my sister), and the music in my niece's room was up so loud that I just couldn't sleep. I was miserable!

I said to the Lord, "Lord, I just came home from doing your work, and I need some peaceful rest. Lord, let not another cuss word come out of my sister's mouth." In an instant, she stopped cussing. As a matter of fact, she tried to cuss. She said "Got dog" instead of the other words. Then I said to the Lord, "Lord, I need peace and quiet." Just as I finished speaking, I heard my niece's footsteps as she ran down the hallway, saying, "Let me turn this music down." Then I said to the Lord, "Lord, thank you for peaceful rest." At last, I heard my nephew say, "Let me go. I'll see y'all later." I told the Lord, "Thank you." Then I immediately went to sleep. You gave me peaceful rest. Thank you, Lord Jesus!

A pair of shoes

I was in a store, and I saw a beautiful black pair of suede heels but not in my size. I looked on *all* the racks. The shoes were not there. Then I said, "Lord, I know they have my size." The next step I took, I stumbled over a pair of black suede shoes. I reached down and picked them up. They were my size. Thank you, Lord!

White sweater

Again, I was in a store, and I saw this white sweater with pieces of silver thread running through it, and I needed it for my outfit for Sunday. I went through all the racks piece by piece. I stopped and placed my hand on the rack as I talked to the Lord. I said, "Lord, I know this sweater is here in my size." Then I looked off to the left. When I looked down at my hand, it was on the rack under my hand in my size. Thank you, Lord Jesus. Praise your holy name.

Missing debit card

One day, I couldn't find my debit card. At this time, I had so many pocketbooks. I didn't know which one to look in, so I looked in all of them. Well, I did not find it. Again, I asked the Lord, "Lord, where is my debit card?"

He said, "Look in your pocketbook." He didn't tell me which one or what color. He simply said, "Look in your pocketbook." *I just knew which one.* So I went to my closet, pulled the pocketbook down, and there it was, in a pocketbook I had already looked in. Praise you, Lord Jesus.

A Dress for the ball

As you can tell by now, I love to shop. So I was at a store again. I saw this black velvet bodice dress with a black-and-maroon, iridescent taffeta skirt—beautiful! I went through every dress on every rack, piece by piece—no dress. I was standing in the middle of the aisle. And I said to the Lord, "Lord, where is this dress?" I turned around, and at the end of two racks where they met end to end, there was the dress just hanging there sideways. It was my size. Lord Jesus, you are so good to me. Thank you, Lord.

Washed my car

I had just gotten off from work on this Sunday morning, got myself ready, and dressed for church. When I got back in the car, I realized how dirty the car was. Now I live only two and a half to three minutes from the church. I said to the Lord, "Lord, this car is so dirty. Make it rain so I can have a clean car." It began to rain, and my car got cleaned. I pulled into the parking lot. And as I was parking, it was still raining. I said to the Lord, "Lord, make it stop raining so I can go into church." Instantly, the rain stopped. I laughed with joy and said, "Thank you, Lord, for being so good to me." By the way, there were no clouds in the sky. It just rained because the Lord did it. Thank you, Lord.

> And let the beauty of the Lord or God be upon us. And establish the work of our hands for us; Yes, establish the work of our hands. (Psalm 90:17 NKJV)

> Ask, and it shall be given you seek, and ye shall find; knock, and it shall be open unto you: (Matthew 7:7 KJV)

And Through It All,
HE KEPT ME

For every one that asked receiveth; and he that seeketh findeth; and to him that knocketh it shall be opened. (Matthew 7:8 KJV)

For thou, Lord, wilt bless the righteous; with favor wilt thou compass him as with a shield. (Psalm 5:12 KJV)

4

Forgiveness

Witness/ex-husband

I heard a sermon on forgiveness: "Don't let bitterness get in your heart. If we don't forgive others, God won't forgive us."

I got on my knees when I got home from work this particular morning and asked the Lord, "Not to let bitterness build up in my heart?" regarding my ex-husband and "to take it away from me." I told him, "I don't have anyone to witness to because I'm working when everybody is sleeping and sleeping when everyone else is working." (My work shift was 11:00 p.m. to 7:30 a.m.)

After prayer, I got in my car and was heading to my mom's house and got on the 826 Expressway. Suddenly, I heard this horn honking repeatedly behind me. I looked in my rearview mirror; it was Jessie, my ex-husband. He was coming up on me so fast from behind me; it was sort of frightening. Then he pulled alongside me. I read his lips ("Pull over") as he gestured with his hand.

He got out of his car and walked back to my car. I rolled down the window, and we greeted each other. That was all I heard him say until after I witnessed to him.

I don't remember all the things I said to him, but I witnessed to him on the side of that expressway for about forty-five minutes about my Lord and Savior. Then I heard myself saying, "I forgive you and Clara for what you did to me."

He said, "I know you're saved."

I asked him, "Would you like to ask Jesus to come into your heart?"

"No, not today," he told me.

I said, "Today is the day of salvation. Tomorrow is not promised to us." His reply was still "no." We said our goodbyes to each other, and I continued on to my mom's house.

When he left, I felt light. It's hard to describe. It was as if something lifted off me (heavy weight, free from bondage, hurt, pain, bitterness), things I did not realize I was carrying around in my heart for all those years. Oh my God! Just think, they had already moved on, and I was still stuck in bondage, in the past. But God delivered me out of them all. I praise your holy name, Lord Jesus. Thank you for delivering me from bondage. Amen. Forgiveness is beneficial for us. Don't let bitterness get into your heart. It can kill you.

Gun to my head
A word of knowledge from "a true prophet"

This word of knowledge was for me, but being a new Christian at the time, I kept saying "but, but…"

My pastor, the late bishop Isaiah S. Williams, had a word of knowledge from the Lord. I could not understand how this man, who did not know me, could tell me something about me that happened years ago, long before I even knew what salvation was, but the Lord knows *all* things.

I was in church with my husband (Alvin), and Pastor was speaking, saying, "There's someone in here who has had a gun put to their head. You didn't do anything wrong." I began to feel queasy, sick to my stomach, and about to throw up. (I told my husband that.) He asked if I wanted him to go up with me. I said no. (Maybe it was someone else). Then Pastor said, "It's been about seventeen years ago." (In my head, I was saying, "I don't know how many years it's been. I'll have to check.") Then he said, "The Lord said you have not forgiven him." Oh my God! I never went up to the altar.

When I got home, I went through all the events that led up to that incident. And after I tallied up all the time, it had happened *exactly* seventeen years ago at that time.

I got on my knees and asked the Lord for forgiveness, for doubting the man of God, and that I forgive the man that had the gun. I also thanked the Lord for showing me that I still had unforgiveness in my heart.

The only person I shared this with was my coworker/mentor, Margaret. She told me, "Yeah, it was you."

Forgiveness is key in our own lives. We can't really move forward without it.

> Many are the afflictions of the righteous: but the Lord delivereth him out of them all. (Psalm 34:19 KJV)

> But if ye forgive not them their trespasses, neither will your Father forgive your trespasses. (Matthew 6:15 KJV)

5

Still, Small Voice— You Asked for That

As I stated earlier, I was so excited about what the Lord was doing and showing me in my life. I just wanted to share with everyone. At the same time, I did not know my friend Belle was building resentment toward me. I thought I was sharing things she had already experienced. She had been saved for over twelve years at that time. I did not know.

I really liked Belle. I used to take her to and from work, Actually, I went about four miles round trip out of my way to do that, never asked her for anything for years. I would even go to her house if I wasn't going to work early enough so she could find another way to work (when her phone was not working, even when I was sick.) One night, I went to pick her up for work, and she was acting like she did not know who I was. When I blew the horn to let her know I was there, she looked out her window and said, "Who is that?"

I said, "Oh! You don't know me now?"

She said, "Oh! That's you, Betty. Cora [another coworker] is picking me up."

I just said, "Oh, okay" and left. When I got to work Cora was already there.

Nevertheless, I just stopped trying to be her friend. Well, she stopped talking to me, so I had no choice.

After a while, a lady named Lisa who worked with us came to me and said, "Let me tell you what Belle and Kenneth are saying about you."

I said, "No, if God wants me to hear it, then he'll let me hear it."

Every night I went to work, Lisa was in my face with the same thing, and my answer was still the same.

About a month later, I was on my way to the chapel when I realized I had left my Bible in the drawer in the unit. I went back for it, and through the doorway, I heard Kenneth saying to Belle, "Who does she think she is? Just got saved and thinks she's holier than thou." Then she said, "Ain't that some 'um think she knows everything." It was obvious they did not see me come in. After I got my Bible, it was *obvious that they saw me* because they became *silent*! (I must have looked like a deer in headlights.) I left, and I did not look back. I just left! I was devastated. Oh my God, I was so hurt. I could not stop the tears from flowing. By the time I got to the chapel, I was a wreck. Thank God, Margaret was there. She prayed for me, and I calmed down some. By the time we got back to the unit, I was okay; however, it was quiet.

The next night I went to work, I was just sitting at my desk, working, and the Lord said to me in that still, small (sweet and gentle) voice, "You asked for that." I knew exactly what he was talking about. I did not know I was actually asking the Lord to let me hear it, but God knows our hearts.

> But the Lord said unto Samuel, Look not at his

countenance, or on the height of his stature; because I refused him: for the Lord seeth not as man seeth; for man looketh on the outward appearance, but the Lord looked on the heart. (1 Samuel 16:7 KJV)

And after the earthquake a fire, but the Lord was not in the fire; and after the fire a still small voice. (1 King 19:12 KJV)

6

Lord, You Give Me the Words to Say

Some months later, Belle approached me and asked if she could talk to me. I said, "Yes." After I agreed, I said, "Lord, I'm not going to try and figure out what she is going to say to me, nor am I going to try to figure out what I'm going to say to her. Lord, you give me the words to say."

I went to the chapel that night, and Belle was already there with Cora. I sat down and asked, "You wanted to talk to me?"

She said, "Yeah, you have a problem with me?"

I said, "No, you're the one who wanted to talk to me." (She began elbowing Cora, but she had fallen asleep.)

She said, "You think you are better than me. You think you know more than me."

I told her, "I have never said or even thought anything like that. You are the one who is saying it. All of that is coming out of your mouth. And out of the abundance of the heart, the mouth speaks." She continued to elbow Cora, but she couldn't wake her up. She had nothing else to say. When our break ended, Cora just woke up.

I believe the Lord put Cora in a deep sleep because she had nothing to do with the situation.

I believe that when we seek the Lord in all his wisdom and speak what he says, we win. Praise the Lord.

Later, she apologized and asked for a favor. I took her home that day, but I told her I would not commit to picking her up and taking her back home again. I also told her that I had shared so much with her and Margaret because they had been saved for so long; I thought they had experienced what I was experiencing already. We talked, but our relationship just was not quite the same. She said she had brought Cora to help her with me. I said, "The Lord put her to sleep."

> And when they bring you unto the synagogues, and unto magistrates, and powers, take no thought how or what thing ye shall answer, or what ye shall say; (Luke 12:11 KJV)

> For the Holy Ghost shall teach you in the same hour what ye ought to say. (Luke 12:12 KJV)

7

Dreams

I have always had dreams and some visions (hard to distinguish at times) ever since I was a child—some good, some scary.

The clouds rolled back

I remember this dream so vividly because it was beautiful. It was as if I was not in my body. I was above my body, looking down at my three-year-old self, lying on the grass in the front yard of my mom's house. I was on my back, in shorts, looking up at the sky, smiling and acting like a child.

Suddenly, the clouds began to roll back, making something like a wide circular hole, and I got a glimpse of the prettiest, bluish-greenish, illuminating sky deep, deep inside.

Moving forward years later and as an adult, I dreamed the same dream with the same layout. In the dream, there was a little cottage in a country-like setting with a lot of windows. There were about seven or eight steps leading up to the front door. It was set in the middle of this large area on pure white sand. We—Belle (one of the sisters from my church), Alice, and me—were standing outside in front of the cottage, facing it. The sky was a pretty medium blue, but the area behind us was dark. There were lots of dark woods and tall dark trees.

Suddenly, the clouds over us began to roll back, forming a circular hole, as if the winds were blowing them back. Inside was deep and bright pure white. At the entrance, there were seven small, white birds flying around with a larger white bird that seemed to be protecting them and keeping them from flying out. It was beautiful!

The light from the sky lit up the area on the ground where we were standing. I looked up and said to them, "Look at those beautiful birds. Look, look." Alice looked up, and she could see those birds and was in awe. I looked at Belle. She had her head down, looking sad, but I kept telling her to look up. This time I turned to look at her; she was gone. Even though I didn't see where she went, I knew she had gone into those dark woods behind us.

Alice and I began calling her, "Belle, Belle, Belle," but she never answered.

Obviously, I did not share this dream with Belle. Later, she was transferred to another unit. I haven't seen or heard from her since. However, every time she comes across my mind, I do pray for her.

The number seven

A voice came to me in this dream and said, "Take this number six, six." Then I heard another voice say "seven," and this same voice said, "Praise the Lord" as my hand raised off the bed on its own. I put my hand down. My hand raised up again all by itself, and again I heard the same voice say, "Praise the Lord," but this time I was awake. As my hand was in the air, I saw a bright green glow around the tips of my fingers. I did praise the Lord!

Man of my dreams

I had a dream about a man whom I believed that God put in my dream so that when I see him, I would know that God sent him. He was tall, about six feet, around 180 to 200 pounds, and dark. He had a round head, thinning hair that was combed back or pushed up in the front, clean cut. He was dressed well, manly, gentlemanly, and filled with Holy Spirit.

Wrong decision

Alvin and I met. We were both part of the homeless ministries at our church. He had all the features, except he did not have the weight yet, and he is 5'11".

One Sunday, after church, he asked me if he could take me out to lunch. I said yes. From there, we went to the movies, dinner, plays, and would sit together in church. For a while, everything was great, then things got out of hand. We took our eyes off the prize, lost focus, and made the wrong decision.

I told him, "We've got to do the right thing before God. We can't do this." So we went our separate ways. He began seeing someone else. Yes, it was hurtful and painful, but that's what it was.

Dr. Gloria "Repent"

I dreamed that I was in a maze and running, trying to get to the exit. A sister from the church, Tonya, was running behind me, trying to catch me because she had a message from Dr. G. I didn't want to hear it, so I kept running and running around in that maze. I finally got to the exit and was about to step out when I turned to see where Tonya was. When I turned back around to step out of the maze, Dr. G was standing just outside, facing me, and she simply said, "Repent."

I did repent and said to the Lord, "Lord, you sent my pastor to me with that message?" Thank you, Lord!

In February the next year, I bought a condo. I asked my niece's boyfriend if he would help me move. He said, "Yes." I called Alvin and asked him if he would help me move; he said, "Yes."

In March, he came by. We talked. Later, we began talking a little more. I shared the dream of Dr. G. with him and how the Lord sent our pastor to me in a dream. In June of that same year, he came over with rings and asked me to marry him. I said, "Yes." In August of that same year, we were married.

The "lighted path"

> Thy word is a lamp unto my feet, and a light unto my path! (Psalm 119:105 KJV)

After we were married, I had this dream/vision/visitation from the Lord. I couldn't tell which it was. But when it happened, I said, "Thank you, Lord, for your visitation." Also, because it was on the same day, one year later, I was baptized with Holy Spirit.

What I saw was a lighted pathway, not lights around the path. The pathway itself was light. And as I was looking down that path, at the end of it was like a doorway, lit up like a steady bright, glowing light in it and through it. One day, I was looking through a catalog, and I saw this small four-by-four-inch painting of that same vision (painted by a well-known Christian painter) resting on an equally small easel that you can sit on a table. Yes, I did buy it, and I still have it. To me, that was my confirmation. I married the right man.

A remarkable dream

My husband, Alvin, and I were at this open type of mall with tall palm trees and beautiful small plants with lights around them and going down the center of this wide four-lane-size walkway. The retail stores had their exquisite displays behind those windows as people were going in and out of their doors.

We were strolling down the walkway, holding hands, making small talk when, suddenly, the eastern sky began to open right in front of us. The brightness and noise of the swirling wind were around us. The dogs were running to and fro, barking like crazy, and at times acting timid. People were coming through the storefront windows and some through the doors as we were all gazing and running toward this spectacular phenomenon in the clouds. Alvin and I were also running and shouting, "Glory! Glory! Glory!" Now we were at the end of the walkway at the mall, and there was a barricade. Just as we stepped over it, our feet left the ground. At the same time, I could see our street and all the houses on it in the neighborhood where we live. We were facing eastward toward the sky where the sun rises. Then I woke up. I just lay there. I was in awe. Hallelujah! Praise to you, Lord God.

I shared it with some of the people from my church family, and one of them said, "Ooh, you had an encounter with God!"

> For as the lightning comes from the east and flashes to the west, so also will the coming of the Son

of Man be. (Matthew 24:27 NKJV)

Then the sign of the Son of Man will appear in heaven, and then all the tribes of the earth will mourn, and they will see the Son of Man coming in the clouds of heaven with power and great glory. (Matthew 24:30 NKJV)

But he, being full of the Holy Ghost, looked up stedfastly into heaven, and saw the Glory of God, and Jesus standing on the right hand of God. (Acts 7:55 KJV)

And said, Behold, I see the heavens opened, and the Son of Man standing on the right hand of God. (Acts 7:56 KJV)

And Through It All,
HE KEPT ME

The prophet that hath a dream, let him tell a dream: and he that hath my word, let him speak my word faithfully. What is the chaff to the Wheat? saith the Lord. (Jeremiah 23:28 KJV)

And it shall come to pass in the last days, saith God, I will pour out my Spirit upon all flesh: and your sons and daughters shall prophesy, and your young men shall see visions, and your old men shall dream dreams. (Acts 2:17 KJV)

Then we which are alive and remain shall be caught up together with them in the clouds, to meet the Lord in the air: and so shall we ever be with the Lord. (1 Thessalonians 4:17 KJV)

8

Healing

Asking God for Direction in My Life

I was not going to share this chapter in my book because it was painful. Actually, I had crossed it out of my rough draft copy on Saturday night before going to bed. I was going to start on a different chapter after I come home from church Sunday. I thought, I kind of felt like Joseph (from the Bible), sharing all his dreams with his brothers, and they threw him in a pit. Well, I was also sharing all my dreams and encounters with Margaret, my friend and mentor, and she didn't take heed to anything that was happening to me. Honestly, I didn't know what was happening to me nor in me because all I knew was they were just my dreams and encounters, and I told them like I always did.

However, before I get into this chapter. We had a visiting pastor on Sunday, and He spoke on this very thing. He was saying, "What are we going to do with the offenses you've got? When life experiences tick you off, you are betrayed. Do you fall into a trap and get bitter? Don't get caught in the trap. God put people in our lives to develop his character in us. Keep your character right in your heart—right, clean, and pure. In other words, use Joseph's story and life as an example of how we should handle traps and still be an effective witness with a pure heart" (Genesis 37:5–36, 44:9–34).

Asking God for direction in my life

I was praying and asking God for the direction of my life. I fell asleep and my hands were tingly, hot, and numb. I kept saying, "My hands are hot and numb" as I kept staring at them.

By now, Margaret and I had formed a small two-man ministry of prayer and healing. We even named it Runners for Christ.

We began going into patients' rooms at the hospital to pray for them (when we were allowed).

My fever broke

The first night we went into an older gentlemen's hospital room, we asked him why he was in the hospital. He said, "My fever is so high. It won't break." I laid my hand on him while Margaret prayed. As soon as she finished praying, "*My fever broke!*" the gentleman shouted with a loud voice. We rejoiced with him and told him it was not us that healed him but Jesus. The following night, we went to his room. He had been discharged. Unfortunately, we never got to do that again.

Now a new young woman transferred to our unit. The ministry, friendship, and mentorship began to strain. Margaret began taking her breaks with her and coming back sometimes fifteen minutes late. That was a problem. When I confronted Margaret about it, the young woman would answer with a smart remark with Margaret smiling and snickering from behind her. Even though we were all Christians, I could feel the prejudice and indifference toward me like a wedge was being driven between us. I was crushed, but I thank God. I can depend on him because he is my friend that sticks closer than a brother (or sister).

Car radiator explosion

One night, after arriving at work, Margaret got a phone call that her son, Keith, was in the emergency room. She asked me to go with her to the emergency room. I went. Then she said to me, "Lay your hands on him while I pray."

I said, "Me?"

"You know you have healing hands, Betty," she said.

I placed my hands on her son while she prayed. He went home with no blisters or scares. Praise the Lord.

Black rotting throat

Even though a wedge had been driven between us, when we needed one another's support and prayer, we did not hesitate.

One afternoon, I was at home. My son, James, came to me and showed me his throat. It was black and looked like it was rotting. We got in the car and went to his doctor's office. They would not see him. After that, we went to two hospitals. They would not see him. He had been dropped from his father's insurance.

We got back home, and my son said to me, "*Mom, pray for me.*" I picked up the phone and called Margaret and told her what was happening. She asked, "Where is he?"

"Right here," I told her.

"Lay your hands on him, and I'll pray." As soon as she finished praying, my son said, "I'll be back."

I said, "Wait until you get better."

"Mom, I'm fine," he said. When he showed me his throat, it was healed. Thank you, Lord Jesus.

White spots

Every day, for about three weeks, there were little white itchy spots all over my torso every time I took a shower. I asked my son if he had been itching, and he said, "Yes." After about the third week, I had had enough! So one morning, after I had showered and itching like crazy, I looked in the mirror and said in a *loud* voice, "*Devil, I don't care what you do to me. I'm still gonna serve my God*!" and I went to bed. When I woke up, all the spots and itching were gone. When my son got home, I asked him, "Are you still itching?"

He said, "*No.*" Thank you, Lord Jesus. Praise your holy name. And they have never returned.

The power of the Lord is in me!

One day, one of my coworkers, Richard, asked me to walk with him to a nearby fast-food shop for a cup of coffee. I went. Oh my! He was very disrespectful toward women. I had to shut him up. Yes, I even went to the supervisor, and he was just as rude and obnoxious with her. I shared it with Margaret and told her, "Don't be snickering and giggling with him. He will embarrass and disrespect you."

I don't know how long after I told Margaret that, I had a dream about Richard, and I shared it with her. The dream was: We were at work and Margaret and Richard, and I were in the unit. Richard was sitting behind me, and every time I looked back at him, it was as if he was looking at something on the floor. About the third time I looked back, I asked him, "What's wrong, and what's on the floor that you keep looking at?" The closer I got to him, the lower he bowed his head to the floor. I heard him chanting something, and I caught him by his neck and began speaking in tongues as fast as I could. In my mind, as I was speaking in tongues, I was saying, "*The power of the Lord is in me*!" Then I saw a bright light, and there was a big *boom*! When I woke up, I was speaking in tongues.

Shortly after I shared the dream with Margaret, this particular night, she and Richard were sitting in the unit, talking and giggling with each other, seemingly having a good time. Then she asked Richard to walk with her to get coffee. I cannot repeat what he said, but I can tell you, it was not nice. All she could do was look at me and drop her head. I did not say a word. I just turned around and continued working.

The party

I remember Margaret and I planned a party for the nurses for nurses week. She said she would purchase the food, and I would pay her for half the cost. I agreed. To make a long story short, I did that, but she did not want to take the money, and it went back and forth for a little while until I shoved the money in her pocket. I found out that she had told the nurses that "she" gave them the party. I was wondering why the nurses were coming from the party only thanking her. I know I'm not invisible.

One of the nurses asked me if I had contributed to the party. Smiling I said, "Yes," thinking she was going to say, "Thank you." That's when she told me Margaret had told all the nurses "she" had given them the party. Boy, that was dirty.

Caught in the trap

In some of the stories in this book I've shared, how in some instances I was beaten up verbally, all the nasty smirks, smart remarks, not wanting to be involved in anything I was a part of, the snickering, and all coming from Christians—I focused on that. I should have focused on the one who can deliver me from all the hate, who loves me unconditionally. I got caught in the trap. Oh my God! One night, one of the doctors came through the doorway just when I was about to take my break. I had my Bible in my hand when he said, "Every time I see you, that book is in your hand. What's in there?" *I was silent*! The very thing I am to share with others, the love of God, did not cross my lips. He never approached me again. I had to ask the Lord for forgiveness and to please put someone before this man so he would know the love of God and that he died for us so his life would be changed.

When I read these scriptures, this doctor was brought back to my remembrance.

> But sanctify the Lord God in your hearts: and be ready always give an answer to every man that asked you a reason of the hope that is in you with meekness and fear: (1 Peter 3:15 KJV)

> Having a good conscience; that, where as they speak evil of you as evil doers, they may be ashamed that falsely accuse your good conversation in Christ. (1 Peter 3:16 KJV)

> But the Comforter, which is the Holy Ghost, whom the Father will send in my name, he shall teach you all things, and bring all things to your remembrance,

> whatsoever I have said unto you. (John 14:26 KJV)
>
> And these signs shall follow them that believe; In my name they shall cast out devils; they shall speak with new tongues: (Mark 16:17 KJV)
>
> They shall take up serpents; and if they drink any deadly thing it shall not hurt them; they shall lay hands on the sick and they shall recover. (Mark 16:18 KJV)

I finally stopped sharing things with Margaret up until she retired. I thought, maybe since she is not around all the other people from work anymore, we could get together and do some work, be about God's business.

I went to her house and told her, "I want my prayer partner back." Well, it seemed like she didn't want to be bothered. We shared small talk, but it felt awkward. However, before I left, she said to me, "You were the real thing." I did not make a comment about that. I told her bye, and I left. I contacted her by phone; she didn't answer. So I left a message for her to call me so we could get together. She texted me back with a message that read, "I'm fine." That was the last communication we had.

I had to forgive them all; otherwise, I would not be able to move forward.

9

Order My Steps
I Will Be at Your Side—
Instructing You, Leading
You, and Guiding You

I have never used the phrase "*clean slate*" ever in my life. I don't talk like that. God *instructed* me to say those words so that I could hear them and recognize them as he *leads* me to this ad booklet that is located in our local newspaper. He *guided* my finger down each column on each page of that booklet until my finger stopped on the words that read, "Need a clean slate?" I didn't know what I was doing or looking for. Nevertheless, it was God honoring his word that he had given me. Praise your holy name, Lord Jesus.

I am not suggesting in any way, shape, or form that anyone file for bankruptcy based on my testimony. I am merely sharing my testimony of the Lord to show how he ordered my steps through this wreck I got myself in. I did not ask God, nor did I even count up the cost before making my decision to purchase a car.

God didn't leave me nor forsook me. He walked me through it. I know sometimes God does not answer right away. But I can truly say to you, this was an urgent matter. And with the sincerity and urgency in my heart, he knew I was going to call on him even before I did, and he answered with the same sincerity and urgency. Thank you, Lord!

$400 a week

I had gotten myself into debt. I'm not saying it was a lot of money; however, it was a lot for me. I began praying about it, and I said, "Lord I'm not going to ask you to cancel my debt. I need a job where I could make

$400 per week." This was in addition to my regular job.

The next day, I was driving down 183rd Street on my way home from my mom's house. An old friend of mine, Andy (whom I had not seen in years), began honking his horn. When I saw him, I thought, *What does he want?* He yelled through the car window, "Pull over." I pulled over, and we were in front of these large tall buildings. He came to my car window and asked, "How ya doing?"

I said, "Fine. How are you?"

Then he said, "You know, they're hiring where I work."

I said, "What kind of work do you do?"

"Insurance," he said.

I said, "Insurance. I don't know anything about insurance!"

"That's okay. They'll train you," he said.

I said, "No."

"They pay $400 a week."

I asked him, "Where do you work?"

As he pointed to one of those tall buildings that were behind him, he said, "Right there."

I got the phone number from him. And when I got home, I called. I spoke with the manager, and he set an appointment for the next day for the interview.

The interview

The next day, I went to the interview, and the manager asked me about my experience. I told him, "I have no experience with insurance." Before he said another word, I told him, "God sent me."

He said, "If God sent you, you got the job." (At the time, I did not know he was a Christian.)

I started the next morning. He did not have anyone to train me, so I was there from 8:00 a.m. until after lunch, then he would send me home. I did make $400 a week just for the few hours a day I was there, and I could have paid off my debt in just a few months. Instead of doing that, I bought a car, and now I was in *deep* debt. I did not ask God, nor did I know how long I could work two jobs. Now I was tired and even more stressed. On top of all my old debt, I now had this car payment.

A clean slate

The Lord said, "I'll be at your side, instructing you, leading you, and guiding you."

I got back on my knees and asked the Lord for forgiveness. I said, "Lord I need a clean slate." I was so deep in sorrow. When the Lord began to speak, I did not hear him. I said, "Lord, I didn't hear you. Please repeat it."

He did, and he said, "I'll be at your side, instructing you, leading you, and guiding you."

I did not hear him speak again during this process, he did exactly what he said he would do.

> Call unto me, and I will answer thee, and show thee great and mighty things which thou knowest not. (Jeremiah 33:3 KJV)

> I acknowledge my sin unto thee, and mine iniquity

> have I not hid. I said, I will confess my transgressions to the Lord; and thou forgavest the iniquity of my sin. Selah. (Psalm 32:5 KJV)
>
> I will instruct thee and teach the in the way which thou shall go: I will guide thee with mine eye. (Psalm 32:8 KJV)
>
> When thou goest, it shall be lead thee; when thou sleepest, it shall keep thee; and when thou awakest, it shall talk with thee. (Proverbs 6:22 KJV)

After hearing his voice, I got a strong urge to pick up this booklet of ads that comes in our local newspaper, and I opened it up. My finger began scrolling down each column on each page until it came to this ad with the heading, "Need a Clean Slate?" With my finger resting on the ad, I said "I need a clean slate." I called the number, and it was a bankruptcy attorney. I made an appointment. I did not know I was looking for an attorney, not to mention a bankruptcy attorney.

I went to see her, and her fee was $500. She needed at least $200 just to get the paperwork started. I not only *did not* have $200 to spare, I no longer had a second job. And on top of all that, I had this new car to pay for, along with all my other bills, and my rent was due.

I took $200 from my rent money and paid the attorney. I went to the rental office and told them I didn't have the rent money. I also told them I get paid in two weeks and if I could pay it then. I don't remember what they said. All I know is, when I got home from work that next morning, I had a notice on my door that, in three days, they would start an eviction notice if I did not pay my rent. Oh my God!

Lord, I need some help!

I got back on my knees, and I said, "Lord, I need some help." When I got up off my knees, I had that strong urge to pick up the telephone book. I immediately turned to the pages where all the different departments were where I worked. My finger began scrolling down each column on each page until it came to the department heading, "Employee Assistance Program." I said in a loud voice, "I'm an employee, and I need some assistance."

God knows where everything is. We just have to open our eyes and see where it is that he is showing us. God does not have to investigate anything. He knows everything.

I called and made an appointment. The next morning after work, I went to the appointment and I took the notice from the rent office with me. After I spoke with a lady there for about two hours, explaining what was happening and that I needed help, she said, "Well let me see," and she left the room. She came back and said, "We can give you two weeks." I was excited. I began asking her what kind of payment arrangement I could make to pay it back. She said, "You don't have to pay it back." I was dumbfounded but happy. "You can come pick up the check in the next three days."

I pulled out that notice from the rent office, handed it to her, and told her, "I need that money now!"

She said, "Oh my God!" She left the room again, and when she came back, she said, "You can pick it up in the morning, and you cannot get any more money within a year."

The next morning, I went and picked up the check, and they also gave me $200 worth of vouchers for a major grocery store. I was leaving the parking garage, and I tell you that when I say I didn't have a dime, I didn't. When I got to the exit booth to pay, all I had was one hundred pennies *exactly*, not a penny more. I handed them to the lady, and boy, she was mad. I could hear her grumbling as she counted them. I didn't look up at her. I didn't say a word. I was so choked up and embarrassed. I just kept looking forward. When she let up the gate, I began to cry and thank the Lord that I had all those pennies because every penny counted. I don't know what she would have done.

I took the check to their bank and cashed it. I paid my rent, got gas, and paid the attorney the balance of the money I owed. She gave me some papers to take home, filled them out, and returned them to her.

Car worth $800

I took the papers home, filled them out, and took them back to her office.

A few days later, she called me and said, "You need to have someone tell you that your car is worth $800 and have them put it in writing." (She was referring to the old car that I had given to my son, not the new one.) In regard to the new car, she said, "I am writing a letter to the corporate office for you to take with you when you return the car."

I got on my knees, and I said, "Lord, I need someone to tell me my car is worth $800." I got the phone book and looked up car dealers and began calling different ones, and I was getting anywhere. My son said, "Mom, why don't you go over there!" (He pointed in the direction where the car dealers were.)

We got in the car, and I drove over to where the car dealers were. At the first one we came to, I stopped because there was a man standing in front of it outside the gate, smoking a cigarette. I asked him, "Do you work here?" (I was pointing to the dealership behind him.)

"Yeah," he said. I asked him, "Can you tell me how much you can give me for my car?"

He said, "Yeah, I'll have to take it for a drive."

I said, "Okay," and my son and I got out of the car and waited for him to drive the car around the block. When he came back. He said, "I can give you $800 for it."

I asked, "Can you put that in writing?"

He said, "Sure!" He took out one of his business cards. On the back, he wrote *the date, the make, the model, and $800. He signed it and gave it to me.* I thanked him and immediately took it to my attorney.

While I was there, she gave me the letter to take to the car dealer's corporate office. I don't know the content of the letter. It was sealed, and she did not give me a copy. I took the car to the corporate office, along with the letter. I have not heard anything from them or anything about the car, not even on my credit report.

A new car

I have that "clean slate" now; and prior to all of this, I had spoken to my sister about moving in with me to help me out.

She said she would. I told her, "Let me get a new car first." She agreed. I needed a new car now because when I gave the car to my son, he must have hit every pothole in the street. The steering wheel was going opposite from the tires. I had to put water in the radiator every day, plus take a gallon with me.

I got on my knees and said to the Lord, "Lord, I know you don't want your child's car to break down at eleven o'clock at night while going to work." My attorney called and said, "You know you can buy a new car."

I said, "I can. I was always told once you file bankrupt, you can't buy anything for years."

"Go get yourself a car."

I went to a dealer, and they turned me down. I called my attorney and told her. She said, "Go to another dealer." So I went to another dealer. I didn't hold anything back about the bankruptcy. Everything I asked for on the car, including the color, I got it, and I drove off that car lot with a brand-new car. Thank you, Lord Jesus.

After I got the car, I called my sister and told her that whenever she was ready to move in, she could. She said, "No, I'm going to stay with Madea.

I said, "Okay" and hung up the phone. I fell back on the bed and said, "Lord, I need a place where I don't have to pay more than $200 per month."

Never say never

I had seen these crime-infested old, dark rundown apartments for years. I would say to myself, "I would never live there." One day (and I don't even know why I was on that street), I was passing by them, and there was a sign outside that read, "Newly Renovated Condos for Sale."

The next day, after I picked up the mats for my new car, I went by those condos, stopped, and went inside just to inquire. I spoke with a young lady, and she told me all about the place. I told her about my situation. She said, "Fill out the application anyway." So I did and gave it back to her. "I'm going to take it back right now," she said. When she left the room, I said, "Lord, you said I can ask anything according to your word in the name of Jesus. You said I could have them." Just as I finished speaking, the lady came back and said, "I spoke with the owner, and he said he would finance it for you." Oh man, I began to praise and thank the Lord right then and there (out loud). Then I asked how much would the mortgage be. She said, "$201.49 per month."

I said, "Thank you, Jesus," and I thanked the lady.

New lease

During the whole process of filing for bankruptcy, I had to sign a new lease, and I didn't want to break it. I had begun to build up my credit. I went back to the condos and explained that to them. The owner agreed and told me he would hold it for me until my new lease was up. Thank you, Lord.

$1,100 down payment

Just before my lease was to expire, I contacted the condo office to tell them and to find out how much I would need for the down payment. Now it had been less than a year since I went to the assistance program at my job. I figured, well I couldn't get any more money from them.

I was on my knees again. I said, "Lord, I need $1,100 to put a down payment on this condo. My lease is almost over." I called the program anyway. I explained the situation to the chaplain that I knew it had not been a year yet, but I needed this money for the down payment on a condo that I was buying. He said, "That's a good cause to me. Come by and pick up the check tomorrow."

"Yes! Praise to you, Lord Jesus," and I am still praising him today.

I bought the condo for $20,000 and lived there for two years. We bought a house and rented the condo for three years before selling it for $39,900. Praise the Lord! Thank you, Jesus.

Listen, God *does not* ask, investigate, look for, consult, inquire, look into, look up, ask for advice from, get advice from, look up information, have a conference to look things over, get professional advice. *He* knows *everything* already! He is God.

1. He knew where money was that belonged to me when I didn't know I even had money.
2. He knew I needed not just an attorney but a bankruptcy attorney. I did not know I needed an attorney at all.
3. He knew I needed a dollar amount for my car. I didn't know the man standing outside the gate, nor did I know the condo owner, but God did.
4. Never say never. We don't know who, what, where, why, when, or how God can/will use anyone or anything to get to us just what we need when we need it.

We just have to ask, trust, and believe that he will do it. Praise your holy name, Lord.

I used to be ashamed to tell this testimony, but the testimony is not about me, it's about the Lord and his goodness, his unconditional love for us. Thank you, Lord, for keeping me and answering my prayers.

> And this is the confidence that we have in him, that, if we ask anything according to his will, he hears us: (1 John 5:14 KJV)

> And if we know that He hears us, whatsoever we ask, we know that we have the petitions that we desired of him. (1 John 5:15 KJV)

> Come unto me, all ye that labour and are heavy laden, and I will give you rest. (Matthew 11:28 KJV)

> Take my yoke upon you, and learn of me; for I am meek and lowly in heart: and ye shall find rest unto your souls. (Matthew 11:29 KJV)

> For my yoke is easy, and my burden is light. (Matthew 11:30 KJV)

In all that I was going through, I never, not once, stopped paying my tithes and giving an offering or doubted God.

> Bring ye all the tithes into the storehouse, that there may be meat in mine house, and prove me now herewith, saith the Lord of hosts, if I will not open you the windows of heaven, and pour you out a blessing, that there shall not be room enough to receive it. (Malachi 3:10 KJV)

And I will rebuke the devourer for your sakes, and he shall not destroy the fruits of your ground; neither shall your vine cast her fruit before the time in the field, saith the Lord of hosts. (Malachi 3:11 KJV)

10

Supernatural—The Blue Armband Miracle

My husband and I took our two youngest grandsons Josiah, three years old, and Jayceon, six years old, to Orlando for five days for their birthdays. At check-in, we were all given armbands. The adults got a yellow one, which was the key to the apartment door, and all the children got blue armbands.

We planned something exciting and different for them for each day. This particular day was *"pool day."* We took the kids to the pool where there was one foot of water. They splashed, ran, slid, jumped, laughed, and just had fun. Then we walked across the patio to the lazy river pool. They were so excited; we had to stop them from running and jumping into the pool. We all walked over to the poolside. I reached down and picked up one of those floating tubes for me and Josiah and stood back up, and he was gone.

I called out to him, and there was no answer. I looked over into the pool and saw this blue armband moving in the water. I took one step along the edge of the pool, and I saw his hand waving. He was floating along the edge of the pool's wall, and the current from the lazy pool was moving him along.

As I jumped into the water (that was when I saw his face), his eyes were open, his mouth was closed, and his hand was waving as if he was saying, "Hey, grandma, I'm right here, just floating in the pool, relaxing and enjoying the sun. He was calm and so innocent. However, he was *completely submerged underwater.*

As I caught him by his arm and yanked him out of the water, I yelled out his name, "*Josiah*!" I held him up with one hand and hit him on his back with my other hand. He threw up and began to cry. I held him and asked him if he was okay. He motioned with his head. "Yes." I laid him on my chest as I stroked his little body, kissed him, told him grandma loved him, and thanked and praised the Lord as we floated around in the lazy river pool.

I began looking at all the pictures we had taken. When I got to the pictures for that day, I noticed something that made my jaw drop. In all of the pictures and videos that were taken that day going to the pool, at the pool, and on the way back to the apartment from the pool, *the armband was on his right arm*. All I could see at first was that blue armband. But Josiah was *not* waving his right arm. Josiah was *waving his left arm because Josiah is left-handed*.

Oh my God! What a miracle-working God. God allowed me to see something that was not there *in the natural* in order to save my baby's life—*a miracle!* I will be forever grateful and thankful to you, Lord. Thank you, Jesus. God also does things supernaturally!

As Josiah always says when he sees or experiences something exciting for the first time, "Ooooh my *dod!* So I say almost the same thing, "Oh my God!" What a miracle-working God. Amen!

> But without faith it is impossible to please him: for he that cometh to God must believe that he is, and that he is a rewarder of them that diligently seek him. (Hebrews 11:6 KVJ)

> Now unto him that is able to do exceeding abundantly above all that we ask or think, according to the power that worketh in us. (Ephesians 3:20 KJV)

> Unto him be glory in the church by Christ Jesus throughout all ages, world without end. Amen. (Ephesians 3:21 KJV)

> Yea, though I walk through the valley of the

And Through It All,
HE KEPT ME

shadow of death, I will fear no evil: for thou art with me; thy rod and thy staff they comfort me. (Psalm 23:4 KJV)

11

Touch My Hand

I was praising and worshipping the Lord and began singing "Precious Lord, Take My Hand." As I reached out to him, I felt a touch on my hand. After I finished, I asked the Lord to "speak to me." I stayed on my knees, but I was still and silent. I heard the Lord say, "My son sits at my right hand, and he is making intercession for you, and I have heard your prayers." Thank you, Lord.

> Who is he that condemneth? It is Christ that died, yea rather, that is risen again, who is even at the

right hand of God, who also maketh intercession for us. (Romans 8:34 KJV)

…and so, In All My Disappointments, Rejections, Betrayals, Dreams, Trials, Tests, Love, Hurt, Pain, Favor, Good Times, Hard Times, Right Decisions, Wrong Decisions, God Loves Me Unconditionally
He Never Left Me nor Did He Forsake Me—And Through It All, He Kept Me

12

The Title of This Book and How It Came to Be

Before I began writing the book, I did not even think about what the title would be. I just began to gather my stories together and put them in order.

One night, I had a dream where I and a group of people were singing a rap-style song. I don't remember the lyrics, but the chorus part was, "He kept me. He kept me." I shared the dream with my husband, and I wrote those words down.

After I began writing the book, I was trying to remember those words, but I couldn't, so I asked my husband. He couldn't remember either. I began looking for that piece of paper. I couldn't find that either.

A few days later, I walked into the room where my husband was, and he asked me, "What's the name of your book?"

I said, "*He Kept Me*." I was in awe because, suddenly, I remembered what I had written down. I said to him, "Oh, that's the name of the song from my dream."

Thank you, Lord Jesus.

I heard someone say, there is a window of opportunity out there for all of us, but it is up to us to go through them. I'm believing God that this is my window. Thank you, Lord!

> But the Comforter, which is the Holy Ghost, whom the Father will send in my name, he shall teach you all things, and bring all things to your remembrance, whatsoever I have said to you. (John 14:26 KJV)

13

―――― ❧ ――――

Prayer for Salvation

You have read my testimonies about my Lord and Savior Jesus Christ, and I believe you want to have a relationship with him also. He is the true and living God, counselor, loving, forgiving, and giving God, Savior, Mighty God, Everlasting Father, Prince of peace, etc.

So…pray these few words and make that happen. Say, Lord Jesus, I repent of my sins and I ask for forgiveness of my sins and cleanse me from all unrighteousness. I believe you died (laid your life down) for me, and God raised you from the dead. Now, you are sitting at the right hand of God our Father, making intercessions for me. I invite you into my heart, take control of my life, and make you my Lord and Savior. Thank you, Lord. Amen.

Now that you have prayed that simple prayer, believed in your heart, and confessed with your mouth Lord Jesus, it is made unto salvation. You are now born again (a child of God). Hallelujah! Amen! Ask the Lord to send you to "a real church." (He may just show it to you.)

> For God so loved the world that He gave His only begotten son that whosoever believeth in Him shall not perish but have everlasting life. (John 3:16 KJV)

> That if thou shalt confess with thy mouth the Lord Jesus, and shalt believe in thine heart that God hath raised him from the dead, thou shalt be saved. (Romans 10:9 KJV)

And Through It All,
HE KEPT ME

For with the heart man believeth into righteousness; and with the mouth confession is made unto salvation. (Romans 10:10 KJV)

In All My Disappointments, Rejections, Betrayals, Dreams, Trials, Tests, Love, Hurt, Pain, Favor, Good Times, Hard Times, Right Decisions, Wrong Decisions, God Loves Me Unconditionally. He Never Left Me nor Did He Forsake Me—And Through It All, HE KEPT ME

About the Author

Betty Bishop-Chambers is a woman with a heart for God who truly loves him and shares the gospel with anyone who will give her their ear. She was raised in Miami, Florida, where she spent most of her life and still resides. Betty is married, a mother of one son, and a grandmother of eight grandchildren. She was a secretary in the newborn intensive care unit at a prominent hospital in Miami for twenty-three years before retiring.

Betty is a peacemaker, humble, warm, easygoing but not a pushover, well respected, respectful, nice, good-hearted, giving, and asking nothing in return. She tries to make complicated things (within her bounds) easier. She is outspoken, kind, and has a love for others. She is now the author of her first book, this book.

CPSIA information can be obtained
at www.ICGtesting.com
Printed in the USA
BVHW031508160323
660599BV00003B/392